D1412425

BALLROOM

By S.L. Hamilton

VISIT US AT ABDOPUBLISHING.COM

Printed in the United States of America, North Mankato, Minnesota.
112010
012011

 PRINTED ON RECYCLED PAPER

Editor: John Hamilton
Graphic Design: Sue Hamilton
Cover Design: John Hamilton
Cover Photo: iStockphoto
Interior Photos: Adam Larkey/ABC via Getty Images-pgs 15 & 23; AP-pgs 2, 3, 4, 5, 6, 11, 13, 17, 18, 19, 20, 21 (top), 24, 25, 26, 27, 28, 30, 31 & 32; Arthur Murray Dance Studio-pg 14 (inset); Corbis-pgs 14, 16 & 22; Getty Images-pgs 9, 21 (bottom) & 23; Granger Collection-pgs 8 (inset), 10 & 12; iStockphoto-pg 1; Library of Congress-pg 7, RKO Radio Pictures/Warner Home Video-Fred Astaire/Ginger Rogers-pg 8; Thinkstock-pg 29.

Library of Congress Cataloging-in-Publication Data

Hamilton, Sue L., 1959-
  Ballroom / S.L. Hamilton.
      p. cm. -- (Xtreme dance)
  ISBN 978-1-61714-729-6
  1. Ballroom dancing. I. Title.
  GV1751.H28 2011
  793.3'3--dc22
                          2010037638

CONTENTS

XTREME

Ballroom dances are a variety of fast and slow couples dances. People dance for fun, but they also compete for prizes.

BALLROOM

"Dancing is moving to the music without stepping on anyone's toes, pretty much the same as life." ~Robert Brault

BALLROOM

Ballroom dancing began with England's elite in the 1700s and 1800s. Over time, the dances grew popular with everyone.

HISTORY

By the 1920s, dance teachers had formalized ballroom dance steps. Couples competed in local ballroom dance contests.

DANCE

Waltz

The Waltz is considered the first ballroom dance. It is performed in a 1-2-3 rhythm pattern. Movements include smooth steps, sweeps, and turns.

Dancing the Ländler.

Fred Astaire and Ginger Rogers were famous Hollywood ballroom dancers in the 1930s and 1940s.

Xtreme Fact

The Waltz grew from the Ländler, a German folk dance. Graceful glides and turns replaced the Ländler's hops and jumps.

STYLES

Viennese Waltz

The Viennese Waltz began in Vienna, Austria. It was performed in country inns and taverns before becoming a ballroom dance. The Viennese Waltz is faster and more lighthearted than the traditional Waltz.

Xtreme Fact

Historically, the Waltz was considered shameful because men held women in their arms. Some parts of Germany and Switzerland banned the dance.

Tango

The Tango was first danced in Spain or Morocco. Spanish immigrants brought the dance style to the Americas in the 1800s. Many Tango styles arose, but the modern Tango is usually credited to dancers from Argentina and Uruguay.

Xtreme Fact Italian actor/dancer Rudolph Valentino made the Tango popular in 1921's *The Four Horsemen of the Apocalypse.*

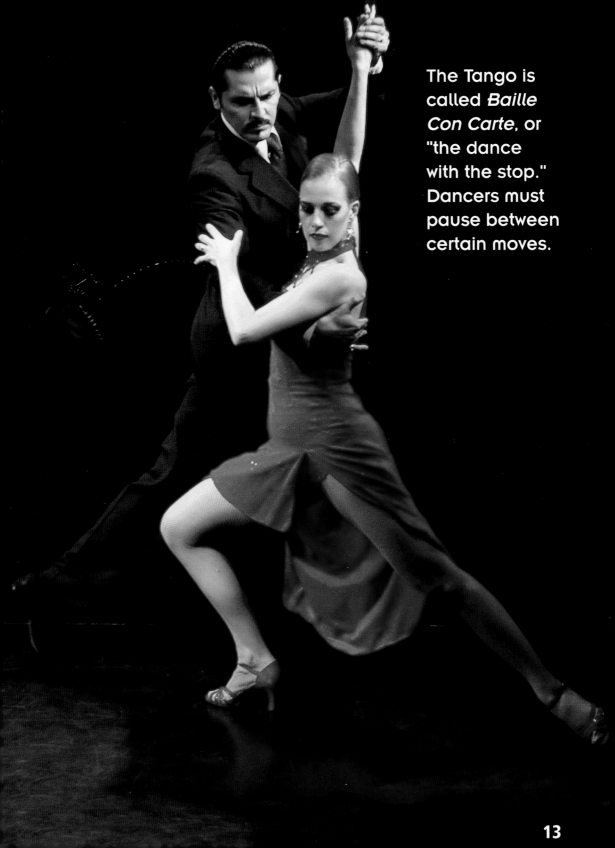

The Tango is called *Baille Con Carte*, or "the dance with the stop." Dancers must pause between certain moves.

13

Foxtrot

Actor Harry Fox created his own dance in 1914, which was first called Fox's Trot. His two slow and two quick trotting steps to ragtime music became known as the Foxtrot. The Foxtrot could be danced to many styles of music. It became one of America's favorite social dances.

"How I Became Popular Overnight!"

"They used to avoid me when I asked for a dance. Some said they were tired, others had previous engagements. Even the poorest dancers preferred to sit against the wall rather than dance with me. But I didn't 'wake up' until a partner left me standing alone in the middle of the floor.

"THAT night I went home feeling pretty lonesome and mighty blue. As a social success I was a first-class failure. At first I wouldn't believe that you could teach by mail because I always had the idea that one must go to a dancing class to learn. But I figured I could risk 10c— especially since you guaranteed to teach me.

How Dancing Made Me Popular

"Being a good dancer has made me popular and sought after. I am invited everywhere. No more dull evenings—no bitter disappointments! My whole life is brighter and happier. And I owe it all to Arthur Murray!

"I was astonished to see how quickly one learns all of the latest steps through your diagrams and simple instructions. I mastered your course in a few evenings and, believe me, I surely did give the folks around here a big surprise when I got on the floor with the best dancer and went through the dance letter perfect. Now that I have the Murray foundation to my dancing I can lead and follow perfectly and can master any new dance after I have seen a few of the steps.

"My sister's family have all learned to dance from the course I bought from you, and it would do your heart good to see how fine her little kiddies dance together after quickly learning from your new method of teaching dancing at home without music or partner."

Arthur Murray, Studio 66
801 Madison Ave., New York City

To prove that I can learn to dance at home in one evening you may send me FIVE FREE LESSONS. I enclose 10c (stamps or coin) to pay for the postage, printing, etc.

Name ....

Address ....

City .... State ....
Also at 150 Southampton Row, London, England

Posed by Miss Ann Forrest, Famous Movie Star, and Arthur Murray, the world's foremost Dancing Instructor

Learn Any Dance in a Few Hours

Whether you want to learn the Fox-trot, One Step, Waltz or any of the new dances, you won't have any trouble in doing it through Arthur Murray's new method. More than 120,000 people have learned to dance by mail, and you can learn just as easily.

Arthur Murray is America's foremost authority on social dancing. Through his new improved method of teaching dancing by mail he will give you the same high-class instruction in your own home that he would give you if you took private lessons in his studio and paid his regular fee of $10 per lesson.

Five Dancing Lessons Free

So sure is Arthur Murray that you will be delighted with his amazingly simple methods of teaching that he has consented for a limited time only to send FIVE FREE LESSONS to all who sign and return the coupon.

These five free lessons are yours to keep— you need not return them. They are merely to prove that you can learn to dance without music or partner in your own home.

Write for the five lessons today—they are free. Just enclose 10c (stamps or coin) to pay cost of postage, printing, etc., and the lessons will be promptly mailed to you. You will receive: (1) The Secret of Leading. (2) How to Follow Successfully. (3) How to Gain Confidence. (4) A Fascinating Fox-trot Step. (5) A Lesson in Waltzing. Don't hesitate. You do not place yourself under any obligation by sending for the free lessons. Write today.

ARTHUR MURRAY
Studio 66, 801 Madison Ave., New York

Xtreme Fact

Instructor Arthur Murray printed and sold Foxtrot dance steps for 10¢ through the mail. It was the first time this was done.

Quickstep

The Quickstep was developed in New York in 1918 when bands played the music for the Foxtrot too fast. The happy Quickstep grew into a fast, carefree, couples dance.

Jive

Jive is a swing dance that is fast and rhythmic. It may have begun with dances created by African slaves brought to the southeastern United States. It might also contain moves created by Florida's Seminole Indians. The dance is acrobatic and fun.

Because Jive is so hard to do, it is often the final dance in a ballroom dance competition.

XTREME

Ballroom dancers must pay close attention to both their partners and the rhythm of the music. Experienced dancers make difficult turns and moves look easy.

MOVES

BALLROOM

Waltzes are usually performed in formal clothing such as ball gowns and tuxes. In contests, dancers are judged on poise and appearance, as well as dancing.

FASHION

Ballroom dances such as the Quickstep and Jive require loose clothing that allows for freedom of movement.

Hair and Shoe Styles

Women ballroom dancers may have long hair, but they keep their locks controlled. Men's hair is well groomed. Formal shoes are standard. Men wear leather or patent leather footwear. Women wear high-heeled sandals or shoes.

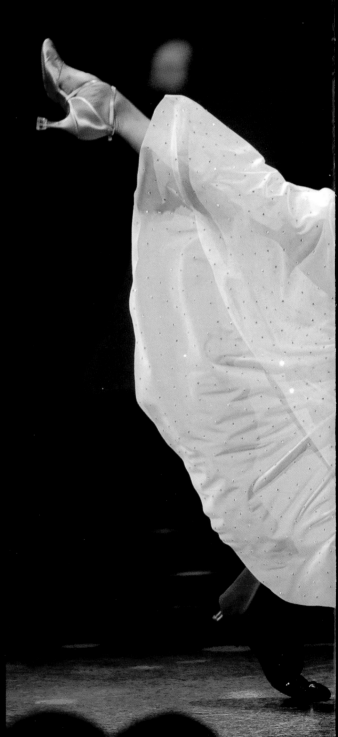

"Remember, Ginger Rogers did everything Fred Astaire did, but backwards and in high heels." ~Faith Whittlesey

Xtreme Quote

LEARN BALLROOM

Many ballroom dances are performed at social events. Because of this, they are commonly taught at dance schools around the world. It is also popular to learn ballroom dance at community centers and health clubs. Instructional DVDs are also available.

DANCING

Xtreme Quote

"Dancing is the art of getting your feet out of the way faster than your partner can step on them." ~Unknown

DANCE

Ballroom dancing contests are known as dancesport. Major dance contests are held throughout the year and around the world.

Dance couples are each assigned a number. Men wear the numbers on their backs. Judges track and score each couple by this number.

CONTESTS

Ballroom dancers must have the correct "look" on their faces. Tango dancers should look serious. Jive dancers should have big smiles.

THE

Americas, The
The lands of North America, South America, and Central America.

Dancesport
Ballroom dancing performed as a sporting contest, instead of for enjoyment. In dancesport, couples or groups are judged on how they are dressed, expressions on their faces, as well as how expertly they perform their ballroom dance or dances.

Elite
People who consider themselves, or are considered by others, to be the richest, most educated, most powerful, or best at something. This is usually a small group of people.

Formal
Dressed up. A way of looking, including clothing, hairstyle, and shoes that would be worn to a special social event, such as a dance or wedding. Not casual.

GLOSSARY

Morocco
A country in northwestern Africa.

Patent Leather
Formal shoes with a shiny surface over the leather.
Men often wear patent leather shoes when dancing.

Poise
To stand up straight, showing calmness and
confidence. To have a graceful manner.

Rudolph Valentino
A famous silent movie actor who lived from 1895 to
1926. He is credited with making the Tango popular
in the United States.

Seminole Indians
Native Americans made up of various Creek Indian
tribes who lived in the area that would become
Florida. It is believed that some of their dance
moves were used to create Jive.

INDEX